A SPECIAL COLLECTION IN *PRAISE* OF

MOTHERS

A HELEN EXLEY GIFTBOOK

EXLEY
NEW YORK · WATFORD, UK

A mother laughs our laughter,
Sheds our tears,
Returns our love,
Fears our fears.
She lives our joys,
Cares our cares,
And all our hopes and dreams
she shares.

JULIA SUMMERS

SOME TOP HELEN EXLEY GIFTBOOKS:

Mothers...	The Love Between Grandmothers and Grandchildren
Sisters...	The Love Between Mothers and Daughters
Thank Heavens for Friends	To a very Special Friend
The Best of Women's Quotations	To a very Special Grandmother

Dedicated to Momtom

Published simultaneously in 1995 by Exley Publications in Great Britain, and Exley Giftbooks in the USA.
12 11 10 9 8 7 6 5

Selection and arrangement © Helen Exley 1995.
ISBN 1-86187-179-1

Words and pictures selected by Helen Exley.
Border illustrations by Kay Johns.
Picture research by Image Select International.
Typeset by Delta, Watford.
Printed in China.

Thanks to Margaret Montgomery for her help with text research.

Exley Publications Ltd, 16 Chalk Hill, Watford, Herts WD1 4BN, UK.
Exley Publications LLC, 232 Madison Avenue, Suite 1206, NY 10016, USA.

Acknowledgements: The publishers are grateful for permission to reproduce copyright material. Every effort has been made to trace copyright holders, but the publishers would be pleased to hear from any here not acknowledged.
MAYA ANGELOU: "Woman Work" from *And I Still Rise* published by Random House, Inc., 1978; RACHEL BILLINGTON: extracts from *The Great Umbilical* published by Hutchinson/Random Century, 1994, reprinted by permission of David Higham Associates Ltd; PEARL S. BUCK: extract from *The Mother* published by Mandarin/Reed International, 1991, reprinted by permission of A.P. Watt Ltd.; KATHARINE BUTLER HATHAWAY: extract from *Mum's The Word* published by North Rocks Press, 1986; OZORA DAVIS: extract from *Mother – A Little Book of Inspiration* published by Brownlow Publishing Company, 1993; MARILYN FRENCH: extract from *The Women's Room* published by André Deutsch Ltd.; MARGUERITE KELLY and ELLA PARSONS: from *Mother – A Little Book of Inspiration* published by Brownlow Publishing Company, 1993; JANE LAZARRE: extracts from *The Mother Knot* published by Virago Press Ltd., 1987; IBARAGI NORIKO: "What a Little Girl Had on Her Mind" from *The Burning Heart* published by The Seabury Press, 1977; GARY PLAYER: extract from *Reflections of a Champion* published by Sidgwick & Jackson/Macmillan Publishers Ltd., 1991; DR BEVERLEY RAPHAEL: extract from *A Celebration of Mothers in Prose and Poetry* published by Michael O'Mara Books 1993 © The Watermark Press 1988; LOUISE ROBINSON BOARDLEY: "Mother, In Sunlight" from *Double Stitch* published by Harper Perennial/HarperCollins USA; CAROL SHIELDS: extract from *Swann* published by Viking Penguin/Penguin Books © 1989 Viking Penguin; MAKSIM TANK: "Mother's Hands" from *Like Water, Like Fire* ed. Vera Rich published by Allen & Unwin; GLORIA VANDERBILT: extract from *Woman To Woman* published by Garden City, Doubleday; MARGARET WILLY: extract from *Every Star a Tongue* published by Heinemann/Reed International.

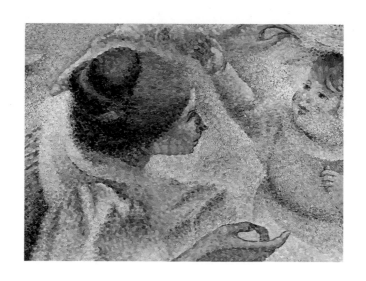

GIFTS

"Look!" you said. And I saw the storm clouds heap and roll and darken and the sky turn blue and the silver lightning tear the dark from top to bottom.

"Look!" And I saw the geese go by, beating their wings against the evening air, and calling to one another as they passed.

"Look!" And I saw the stillness of a lake erupt to a shimmering of fishes, chasing the crumbs you'd thrown.

"Look!" And I saw a sky peppered with stars. And the glitter of frost on every blade of grass.

"Look!" And I saw the little things I might have missed. The pods of scarlet pimpernel, the fine-wire legs of a sociable robin, and his understanding eye, the whirls in the ear of a kitten, and the dew-spangled webs of spiders strewn across the hedge, the dip and dart of damselflies, the scampering of beetles, the quiver of a mouse's whiskers, the snub green nose of a hyacinth shoving through the soil.

You gave me food and warmth and love.

And you gave me stars.

ROSANNE AMBROSE BROWN

I sit on his bed and smooth his hair, pull the covers up, kiss him wet and long. Here it is, I think, sighing with relief. Here is the mother-feeling they talk about. It comes when your child is old enough to love you back, when you have known him for a while, when you are no longer physically suffering, when you have grown used to your life's changes, when you have no choice but to love him – more than a puppy you watched being born, more than a roomful of plants you shine fluorescent lights upon each evening, more than a long beautiful poem you have written over and over, adding a word and erasing a thought and finally knowing that the last line must be <u>that</u>, that phrase you have been looking for all over the place and finally it comes in a flash and you wonder, later when you read it to a friend, now where did I get that from? You love the child more. I had held my infant hour after anguished hour, worrying, Where are those feelings? And now, here they are at last.

I am soothed. I walk back to the kitchen and touch his lunch box, all ready, then into the living room where I stroke, just once, my desk, wondering. Then I go to sleep.

JANE LAZARRE, FROM *THE MOTHER KNOT*

Mothers are the pivot on which the family spins.
Mothers are the pivot on which the world spins.

PAM BROWN

The mother is the most precious possession of the nation, so precious that society advances its highest well-being when it protects the functions of the mother.

ELLEN KEY

A mother is she who can take the place of all others but whose place no one else can take.

CARDINAL MERMILLOD

$\mathcal{T}$he actual experience of being a mother

is one of the most fulfilling I've ever had.

Pregnancy was the most continuous happiness

I've known. Each time I've experienced birth

there's been an overbearing feeling of loss,

in the hospital right after the baby's birth,

when the baby would be taken into the nursery.

And then the greatest flooding of joy

when the baby would be brought back to me.

GLORIA VANDERBILT, FROM *WOMAN TO WOMAN*

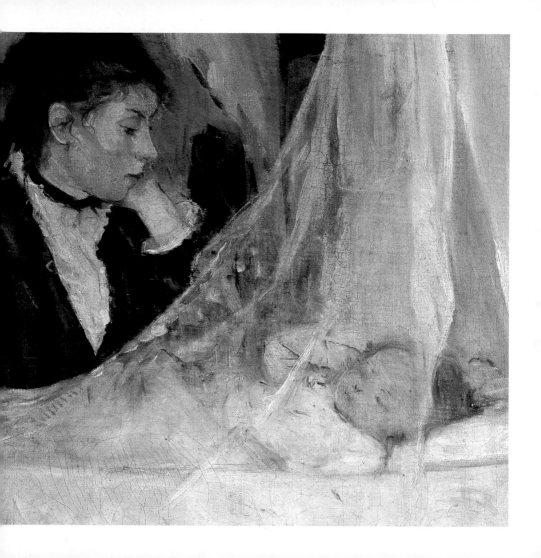

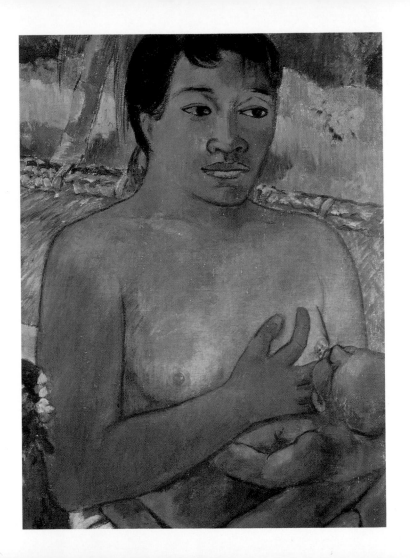

WOMAN WORK

I've got the children to tend
The clothes to mend
The floor to mop
The food to shop
Then the chicken to fry
The baby to dry
I got company to feed
The garden to weed
I've got shirts to press
The tots to dress
The cane to be cut
I gotta clean up this hut
Then see about the sick
And the cotton to pick.

Shine on me, sunshine
Rain on me, rain

Fall softly, dewdrops
And cool my brow again.

Storm, blow me from here
With your fiercest wind
Let me float across the sky
'Till I can rest again.

Fall gently, snowflakes
Cover me with white
Cold icy kisses and
Let me rest tonight

Sun, rain, curving sky
Mountain, oceans, leaf and stone
Star shine, moon glow
You're all that I can call my own.

MAYA ANGELOU

A SMALL SALUTE

Let's have a roll of drums here, and a toot of trumpets.
Let's have a cheer.
For all the mothers going it alone – whose partners
have run or walked away and left them on their own,
with one or two – or three or four or five – children to
cope with.
Who have to cry at night. Or wail in the garden shed.
Whose smiles make Pagliacci seem an amateur.
Whose rages must only bubble inwardly and never
spill over to scald the kids – who have enough to bear.
Who sometimes fail – and hate themselves for failing.
Who live in dread of concerned officialdom, bills, the
wearing-out of shoes.
Who pull themselves together, find new freedoms and
splendid friendships. Who lay out their money with
wisdom and panache, delight in Sales, discover treats
that do not cost a bean, keep joy alive, their children
warm and fed.
– And certain of their love.

PAM BROWN

A MOTHER'S CREED

I believe in the eternal importance of the home as the
    fundamental institution of society.

I believe in the immeasurable possibilities of every boy
    and girl.

I believe in the imagination, the trust, the hopes and ideals
    which dwell in the hearts of all children.

I believe in the beauty of nature, of art, of books, and
    of friendship.

I believe in the satisfactions of duty.

I believe in the little homely joys of everyday life....

OZORA DAVIS

As he drew the milk out of me, my inner self seemed to shrink into a very small knot, gathering intensity under a protective shell, moving away, further and further away, from the changes being wrought by this child who was at once separate and a part of me. Frightened that he would claim my life completely, I desperately tried to cling to my boundaries. Yet I held him very close, stroked his skin, imagined that we were still one person.

I turned to that self inside of me, that girlwoman who had once been all I needed to know of myself, whom I had fought to understand, to love, to free – I turned to her now and I banished her. … She who had been my life, whom I knew I had to nourish daily in order to be fed in return, hid for weeks, hoarding her gentleness and her strength, placing no gifts in my outstretched hands.

JANE LAZARRE, FROM *THE MOTHER KNOT*

Isn't this strange? Isn't this wonderful?
Look at the lighting – see how it changes
– look at the rainbow caught up in the leaves.
Country or city street, you were beside me.
Showing me wonders that others
    had missed.

PAM BROWN

*A mother is not a person to lean on,
but a person to make leaning unnecessary.*

DOROTHY CANFIELD FISHER

There is so much to teach, and the time goes so fast.

ERMA BOMBECK

It will be gone before you know it.
The fingerprints on the wall appear higher and higher.
Then suddenly they disappear.

DOROTHY EVSLIN

Children and mothers never truly part –
Bound in the beating of each other's heart.

CHARLOTTE GRAY

You never realize how much your mother loves you
till you explore the attic – and find every letter
you ever sent her, every finger painting, clay pot,
bead necklace, Easter chicken, cardboard Santa Claus,
paperlace Mother's Day card and school report
since day one.

PAM BROWN

MOTHERS HANDS

The earth has kissed them indeed,
With sandy lips it has kissed them,
With the grain-ears;
And with the noon-heat, the winds and the rain-showers
The sky has kissed them.

Such toil of spinning
Through sleepless nights has drunk from them
Freshness of morning;
So many times have they kindled the day-break,
Stars over us

How many are there today,
Seen on them, dark and scored deeply,
Scars, lines and wrinkles,
They are the traces forever imprinted
On our harsh pathway.

And yet, whenever
the family gather at home,
And mothers hands rest on the table,
As if from the sun, light from them fills the house with its
*   radiance,*
Fills the heart.

MAKSIM TANK

Motherhood has its marvelous power, and in it is blended pain and joy, at once the deepest and the most cleansing influence in the world. That it brings joy no one can doubt who sees the mutual love of mother and child; that there is pain in it all must recognize. Perhaps its chief grace lies in the fact that it is a ministry in which in a unique degree there is blended purposeful self-sacrifice with the confident expression of love in its purest quality. Motherhood is the paradox of life; in its fear and its resolution, its giving and receiving, at once the suppliant for our protection and the imperious monarch of our lives, it bids men pay their homage to virtue.

FROM THE *NEW YORK TIMES*, MAY 10, 1929

𝕐*ou, who were once simply human, have, by motherhood, been deified.*

But only for a little while.

For the child grows in understanding day by day and the gilding fades – and soon, your child will see you lack omniscience, infallibility, the power to change the world. And the first, last certainty of life is gone.

It is sadness that has come to all of us, this loss of certainty.

But we must let it go if we are to find each other, to love one another as we are – ordinary, flawed, confused – and all the dearer in our frailty.

PAM BROWN

All the time the two children had followed her as best they could, although she moved as she would without stopping for them. Now they clung to her trousered legs, whimpering and crying. She stooped and lifted the younger one into her arms, and leading the older by the hand, she took them into the house and barred the door fast. … However impatient she might be in the day, however filled with little sudden angers, at night she was all tenderness – passionate tenderness to the man when he turned to her in need, tender to the children as they lay helpless in sleep, tender to the old woman if she coughed in the night and rising to fetch a little water for her, tender even to the beasts if they stirred and frightened each other with their own stirring, and she called out to them, "Be still – sleep – day is a long way off yet –" and hearing her rough kind voice even they were quieted and slept again….

… Heavily and deeply they all slept, and if the dog barked in the night they all slept on except the mother, for to them these were the sounds of the night. Only the mother woke to listen and take heed and if she needed not to rise, she slept again, too.

PEARL S. BUCK, FROM *THE MOTHER*

Mother is the heartbeat in the home; and without her, there seems to be no heart throb.

LEROY BROWNLOW, FROM
FLOWERS FOR MOTHER

A woman has a right to joy and pride and contentment if her children have grown up courteous and kind, honest and loving.

She needs just a little applause, all of her own. For her cake making, her embroidery, her flower arrangements – her race-track driving, sky-diving, golf. Her newspaper articles, racing, tennis, riding, campaigning. Her painting, scholarship and acrobatics. Her ability to loop the loop and tap dance.

Viva Mum!

CHARLOTTE GRAY

A TRIBUTE TO MOTHER

Faith that withstood the shocks of toil and time:
Hope that defied despair
Patience that conquered care;
And loyalty, whose courage was sublime;
The great deep heart that was a home for all –
Just, eloquent and strong
In protest against wrong;
Wide charity, that knew no sin, no fall;
The Spartan spirit that made life so grand,
Mating poor daily needs
With high heroic deeds,
That wrested happiness from Fate's hard hand.

LOUISA MAY ALCOTT

She had seen their birth and the birth of her love for them as miraculous, but it was just as miraculous when they first smiled, first sat up, first babbled a sound that resembled, of course, mama. The tedious days were filled with miracles. When a baby first looks at you; when it gets excited at seeing a ray of light and like a dog pawing a gleam, tries to capture it in his hand; or when it laughs that deep, unselfconscious gurgle; or when it cries and you pick it up and it clings sobbing to you, saved from some terrible shadow moving across the room, or a loud clang in the street, or perhaps, already, a bad dream: then you are – happy is not the precise word – filled.

MARILYN FRENCH, FROM *THE WOMEN'S ROOM*

I never thought that you should be rewarded for the greatest privilege of life.

MARY ROPER COKER,
ON BEING CHOSEN
"MOTHER OF THE YEAR," 1958.

[My mother] died almost fifty years ago but I have to admit she has never really left me. Even now I can still remember her vividly. I remember her voice; the things she told me. I can see every line and characteristic of her face. And she has remained the most important influence on my life. All that I am and all that I have become is in some way a tribute to her. It has been a means for me, as it were, to settle some unfathomable debt.

GARY PLAYER, FROM *REFLECTIONS OF A CHAMPION*

Being a mother is an excitement and enticement and a growth. It is the possibility that haunts and delights the young girl as she grows to womanhood. It is a part of the fantasy, both her longing for it and her fear of it. The months of pregnancy highlight all the richness of the remembered and internalized experience about mothering. The birth itself brings forth the baby, until now a fantasy, into reality. This real baby is a constant changing, crying, knowing being, and for me the delight of this experience has been one of the most important parts of my life as a woman.

DR. BEVERLEY RAPHAEL

I love being a mother...I am more aware. I feel things on a deeper level. I have a kind of understanding about my body, about being a woman.

SHELLEY LONG

The greatest battle that ever was fought –

Shall I tell you where and when?

On the maps of the world you will find it not:

It was fought by the mothers of men.

JOAKUIN MILLER

The appealing sweetness given to the baby of the species, whether human, monkey or kangaroo, is nature's guileful way of enslaving the mother. Most mothers...although remaining aware of "the sentence of motherhood", manage to concentrate on the rewards. These range from the sheer fun of a gurgling, rolling, squeaking plaything in the home, to the passionate intensity of the love which many mothers feel for their babies.

RACHEL BILLINGTON, FROM *THE GREAT UMBILICAL*

Mothers have as powerful an influence over the welfare of future generations as all other earthly causes combined.

JOHN S.C. ABBOTT

Everybody knows that a good mother gives her children a feeling of trust and stability. She is their earth. She is the one they can count on for the things that matter most of all. She is their food and their bed and the extra blanket when it grows cold in the night; she is their warmth and their health and their shelter; she is the one they want to be near when they cry. She is the only person in the whole world or in a whole lifetime who can be these things to her children. There is no substitute for her. Somehow even her clothes feel different to her children's hands from anybody else's clothes. Only to touch her skirt or her sleeve makes a troubled child feel better.

KATHARINE BUTLER HATHAWAY

MOTHER, IN SUNLIGHT

I tugged at your skirt, and you smiled.

You stood in sunlight
Near the coal stove
A black iron heating,
A black iron slicking wrinkles
On percale dresses and starched white shirts.
You stood in sunlight
Sweat dripping down your brow.

I think of the hours you spent
To make our world sparkle.

LOUISE ROBINSON-BOARDLEY

...*N*ever was a woman more richly mother than this woman, bubbling over with a hundred little songs and scraps of gay nonsense to beguile a child from tears, and filled with wayward moods as she was, yet her hands were swift to tenderness and care and quiet brooding tending when need arose. Never was she a more perfect mother than during the summers on the mountain top when she could give herself freely to her children. She led them here and there in search of beauty, and she taught them to love cliffs and rugged rocks outlined against the sky, and to love also little dells where ferns and moss grow about a pool. Beauty she brought into her house too and filled the rooms with ferns and flowers.

PEARL S. BUCK, FROM *THE EXILE*

The love of husbands and wives may waver; brothers

and sisters may become deep-rooted enemies; but a mother's

love is so strong and unyielding that it usually endures all

circumstances: good fortune and misfortune, prosperity

and privation, honor and disgrace. A mother's love perceives

no impossibilities.

PADDOCK

Children, ay forsooth,
They bring their own love with them when
they come...

JEAN INGELOW

In the sheltered simplicity of the first days
after a baby is born, one sees again the
magical closed circle, the miraculous sense
of two people existing only for each other.

ANNE MORROW LINDBERGH

Making the decision to have a child – it's
momentous. It is to decide forever to have
your heart go walking around outside
your body.

ELIZABETH STONE

Becoming a mother makes you the mother of all children. From now on each wounded, abandoned, frightened child is yours. You live in the suffering mothers of every race and creed and weep with them. You long to comfort all who are desolate.

CHARLOTTE GRAY

*There is in all this world
no fount of deep, strong,
deathless love,
save that within
a mother's heart.*

FELICIA HEMANS

*Before becoming a mother
I had a hundred theories
on how to bring up children.
Now I have seven children
and only one theory:
love them,
especially when they least deserve
to be loved.*

KATE SAMPERI

Motherly love is not much use if it expresses itself only as a warm gush of emotion, delicately tinged with pink. It must also be strong, guiding and unselfish. The sweetly sung lullaby, the cool hand on the fevered brow, the Mother's Day smiles and flowers are only a small part of the picture. True mothers have to be made of steel to withstand the difficulties that are sure to beset their children.

RACHEL BILLINGTON, FROM *THE GREAT UMBILICAL*

Motherhood brings as much joy as ever, but it still brings boredom, exhaustion, and sorrow too. Nothing else ever will make you as happy or as sad, as proud or as tired, for nothing is quite as hard as helping a person develop his own individuality especially while you struggle to keep your own.

MARGUERITE KELLY AND ELIA PARSONS

I saw pure love
when my son looked at me,
and I knew that I had to
make a good life for
the two of us....

SUZANNE SOMERS

We want to please our mothers, emulate them, disgrace them, oblige them, outrage them, and bury ourselves in the mysteries and consolations of their presence. When my mother and I are in the same room we work magic on each other: I grow impossibly cheerful and am guilty of reimagined naiveté and other indulgent stunts, and my mother's sad, helpless dithering becomes a song of succour. Within minutes, we're peddling away, the two of us, a genetic sewing machine that runs on limitless love. It's my belief that between mothers and daughters there is a kind of blood-hyphen that is, finally, indissoluble.

CAROL SHIELDS, FROM *SWANN*

The greatest moral force in history is motherhood. Childhood is directed by its love; youth is kept pure and honourable by its sweet dominance; and mature age finds its influence regnant, shaping character even to the end. Mother is the title of woman's supreme dignity.

FROM *THE TIMES*, FEBRUARY 1929

She is my first, great love. She was a wonderful, rare woman – you do not know; as strong, and steadfast, and generous as the sun. She could be as swift as a white whip-lash, and as kind and gentle as warm rain, and as steadfast as the irreducible earth beneath us.

D.H. LAWRENCE

...to bear you I had to look on death. To nurture you
I had to wrestle with it. Death fought with me for you.
All women have to fight with death to keep their children.
Death, being childless, wants our children from us.
Gerald, when you were naked I clothed you, when you
were hungry I gave you food. Night and day all that long winter
I tended you. No office is too mean, no care too lowly
for the thing we women love – and oh! how I loved you.
Not Hannah, Samuel more. And you needed love,
for you were weakly, and only love could have kept you alive.
Only love can keep any one alive.

OSCAR WILDE, FROM *A WOMAN OF NO IMPORTANCE*

TO ANY MOTHER

There seemed to be something huge and important to say;
But somehow, then, we could never think of the words.
Anyway, they would keep, so it did not matter,
And there would be time and time enough to remember;
So we laughed as the years flew over our heads like birds.

And then, one day, we remembered them; ran all the way,
Breathless came running, and beat and called at your door:
At the door of a house whose silence and emptiness mocked us,
For you had slipped out the back way, quite quietly, leaving
"I love you, and thank you," unneeded, unsaid, ever more.

MARGARET WILLY

It is the nightly custom of every good mother after her children are asleep to rummage in their minds and put things straight for the next morning, repacking into their proper places the many articles that have wandered during the day....

When you awake in the morning the naughtiness and evil passions with which you went to bed have been folded up very small and placed at the bottom of your mind; and on top, beautifully aired, are spread out your prettier thoughts, ready for you to put on.

J.M. BARRIE

My mother

You're always there in my thought. You always will be there. Your gifts have not been things, although you always gave your most precious things, too. Your gifts have been your constancy, your laughter, your enthusiasm (especially your over-enthusiasm!), the very richness, the festivals, of life.

And you have always been true. That is the essence in my thought.

H.M.E.

How many thousands of heroines there must be now, of whom we shall never know. But still they are there. They sow in secret the seed of which we pluck the flower, and eat the fruit, and know not that we pass the sower daily in the streets.

One form of heroism – the most common, and yet the least remembered of all – namely, the heroism of the average mother. Ah! When I think of that broad fact, I gather hope again for poor humanity; and this dark world looks bright – this diseased world looks wholesome to me once more – because, whatever else it is not full of, it is at least full of mothers.

CHARLES KINGSLEY

WHAT A LITTLE GIRL
HAD ON HER MIND

What a little girl had on her mind was:
Why do the shoulders of other men's wives
give off so strong a smell like magnolia;
or like gardenias?
What is it,
that faint veil of mist,
over the shoulders of other men's wives?
She wanted to have one,
that wonderful thing
even the prettiest virgin cannot have.

The little girl grew up.
She became a wife and then a mother.
One day she suddenly realized;
the tenderness
that gathers over the shoulders of wives,
is only fatigue
from loving others day after day.

IBARAGI NORIKO

You move about your garden, holding your grandchild by the hand, watching her feather-touching the shining flowers, the veined, serrated leaves – peering to see the patternings of form and light, breathing in the scent.

And I am little again, the heavy crimson poppies nodding over me. I feel my hand held safe in yours and hear again the litany of lovely names, and the gentle sounds of a summer I had thought long lost.

For no good thing ever vanishes. It is carried forward from generation to generation.

PAM BROWN

ACKNOWLEDGEMENTS

Exley Publications is very grateful to the following individuals and organisations for permission to reproduce their pictures. Whilst all reasonable efforts have been made to clear copyright and acknowledge sources and artists, Exley Publications would be happy to hear from any copyright holder who may have been omitted.

Cover: **Les Coquelicots,** *Claude Monet (1840-1926),* Musée d'Orsay, Paris, AKG-Berlin.

Title Page: **Peasant family from Kalenberg,** © 1995 Adolf Wissel, (1939), Edimedia, Paris.

Pages 6/7: **Winding the Wool,** © 1995 Alfred Carlton Smith *(1853-1946),* by courtesy of Haynes Fine Art, Broadway, Fine Art Photographic Library.

Page 8: **Mother and child,** *Henri Edmund Delacroix Cross (1856-1910),* Fine Art Photographic Library.

Page 10: **A Portrait of Marian Hartford and her son Stuart,** *Alexander Rossi (fl.1870-1903),* Bonhams, London, The Bridgeman Art Library.

Page 12: **Hide and Seek,** *Paul Edouard Rosset-Granger (b.1853),* Musée des Beaux-Arts, Marseilles, The Bridgeman Art Library.

Page 14/15: **The Cradle,** *Berthe Morisot (1841-1895),* Musée d'Orsay, the Bridgeman Art Library.

Page 16: **L'effrande,** *Paul Gauguin (1848-1903),* Bulloz.

Page 19: **"Buy a bunch of violets, snowdrops or primroses",** *George Morton (fl.1879-1904),* Fine Art Photographic Library.

Page 21: **Gabrielle and Jean,** Pierre Auguste Renoir (1841-1919), *Musée d'Orsay, Paris.* By courtesy of Giraudon/The Bridgeman Art Library.

Page 22: **Springtime,** *Sir George Clausen (1852-1944),* Christie's, London, The Bridgeman Art Library.

Page 24/25: **Near Weybridge, Surrey,** *Edmund George Warren (1834-1909),* Fine Art Photographic Library.

Page 26: *Mark Graham,* The Image Bank.

Page 29: **The Apple Peeler,** *Gerard Ter Bosch,* Kunsthistorisches Museum, Vienna. © Erich Lessing, Art Resource New York.

Page 31: **Mother and Child,** © 1995 Ditz (living artist), The Bridgeman Art Library.

Page 33: **The Foundling,** *Frederick Cayley Robinson (1862-1927),* Leamington Spa Museum and Art Gallery, Warwick, The Bridgeman Art Library.

Page 35: **La Vendemmia,** *Gioli Francesca (1849-1922),* Galleria d'Arte Moderna, Florence, Scala.

Page 36/37: **Musikunterricht,** © 1995 Ernst Hassebrauk (1905-1974), Dresden, Gemaldegalerie, New Meister, AKG-Berlin.

Page 38: **Melissa's Dinner,** *William Dring (b.1904),* Atkinson Art Gallery, Southport, Lancs., The Bridgeman Art Library.

Page 41: **Album du Voyage au Maroc,** *Eugene Delacroix (1798-1863),* Giraudon.

Page 43: **Mother with Child,** *Pierre Auguste Renoir,* National Gallery, Edinburgh, Scotland, Scala.

Page 44/45: **The Train in the Country,** *Claude Monet (1840-1926),* Musée d'Orsay, Paris, Giraudon/The Bridgeman Art Library.

Page 47: *Francesco Gioli,* Gallery of Modern Art, Florence, Scala.

Page 48: **Mother and Child,** © *Norman Hepple (1908-1994),* City Museum and Art Gallery, Stoke-on-Trent, The Bridgeman Art Library.

Page 51: **Algerian Mother,** *Karl Erich Muller (b.1917),* Dresden, Gemaldegalerie, New Meister, AKG-Berlin.

Page 53: **Motherhood,** *Louis Emile Adan (1839-1937),* Waterhouse and Dodd, The Bridgeman Art Library.

Page 54: **The Family,** *Bernard Fleetwood Walker (b. 1892),* City Museum and Art Gallery, Stoke-on-Trent, The Bridgeman Art Library.

Page 56: **Portrait of Madame Coste** detail, *Jean Jalabert (1815-1900),* Musée des Beaux Arts, Carcassone, Edimedia, Paris.

Page 58/59: **Butterflies,** *Charles Sims (1873-1928),* Fine Art Photographic Library.

Page 61: **Feeding the Young,** © 1995 Jean-Francois Millet (1814-1875), Musée des Beaux-Arts, Lille, Giraudon/The Bridgeman Art Library.

Page 63: **The Wet Nurse,** *Alfred Roll (1846-1919),* Musée des Beaux-Arts, Lille, Giraudon/The Bridgeman Art Library.

Page 64/65: **L'inscrizione al Kolkhoz,** *Fratelli Tkaciov,* Tret'jakov Gallery, Moscow, Scala.

Page 66: **Bathtime,** *Alfred Edward Emslie,* Fine Art Photographic Library.

Page 69: **Tender Grace of a Day that is Dead,** *Walter Langley (1852-1922),* Oldham Art Gallery, Lancs., The Bridgeman Art Library.

Page 70: **Apron Strings,** *Frederick Morgan,* Fine Art Photographic Library.

Page 73: **Christening in Tanum Church,** *Harriet Backer (b.1845),* Masjonalgalleriet, Oslo, The Bridgeman Art Library.

Page 75: **Ia Orana Maria,** *Paul Gauguin (1848-1903),*

Metropolitan Museum of Art, New York, © Erich Lessing.

Page 76/77: **Sentiero a Saint-Tropez,** *Henry Charles Manguin (1874-1943),* Ermitage Museum, St Petersburg, Scala.

Page 78: **La Blanchisseuse,** *Honore Daumier (1808-1879),* Musée d'Orsay, Paris, AKG-Berlin.

Page 80: **Woman and Child in a Meadow,** © 1995 Hector Caffieri *(1847-1932),* Bonhams, London, The Bridgeman Art Library.

Page 82/83: **Mimosas, Anemones and Foliage in a Blue Vase,** *Odilon Redon (1840-1916),*

Musée du Petit Palais, Paris, Lauros/Giraudon.

Page 85: **A Point of Interest,** *Elizabeth Stanhope Forbes (1859-1912),* David Messum Galleries, London and Beaconsfield, The Bridgeman Art Library.

Page 87: **My Family,** *Martinos Soryan (1929),* Tret'jakow Gallery, Moscow, Edimedia, Paris.

Page 88/89: **A Family Sing-Song,** *Brita Barnekow,* by courtesy of Burlington Paintings, London,

The Bridgeman Art Library.

Page 90: **Tea in the Garden,** *Thomas James Lloyd (1849-1910),* Fine Art Photographic Library.

Page 92: **Camille Monet with Child in the Garden at Argenteuil,** *Claude Monet (1840-1926),* Boston Museum of Fine Arts, AKG-Berlin.